VOLUME 1

The Donald – Campaign

The Real Donald

VOLUME 1

CHAPTER 1

The Donald – Campaign Announcement 12/05/2015

Dear World,

I am pleased to announce the presidential candidacy of The Donald. This is not the Donald you all know of. This a more well-spoken, better-mannered, fighter-of-justice, and sqausher-of-unreasonability Donald. The only common characteristic is the comb-over. Oh, and possible lack of priority for political correctness. This Donald's expression of thought, however, is always well received.

So without further ado, I present the official campaign platform. Make your vote matter and vote for The Donald! Enjoy reading!

Message 11/29/15

To My Honorable, Non-Biased Campaign Staff:

After much deliberation, (3.14 minutes) and receiving feedback from my "feasibility study"; with amazing support (7 people) and beckoning requests (4 people), I have decided to throw my hat in the ring and become another (somewhere above 10) candidate for President.

The theme for my campaign is "Will the Real Donald, please stand up."Please watch this video to learn how to tell the difference between "fake and real."

https://www.youtube.com/watch?v=v3bSwCJD1_8.
(Make sure you start at the beginning of the video)

**My motto is: " If you don't offend me,
I won't offend you"**

My campaign vehicle is: "Rambo One"

Rambo One (our family vehicle of 25 years) is the Official Presidential Campaign vehicle (see below). What do you think? If you like it, then good. If you don't, then it doesn't matter what you think. If this vehicle ever breaks down, my back-up is the cow that kicked Mark (our favorite brother-in-law), which will be pulling Rambo One from town to town.

I plan to visit every "little town" in America, give away Playskool "Cell Phones" from Toys R Us. If you vote for me once you will receive a a free Chick Fil A sandwich and if you vote for me twice, you get waffle fries also. If Mark and Jen (wife of the favorite brother-in-law) can convince all of the great citizens of Muleshoe to vote for me, I will have a high likelihood of winning the national election. I will visit Oshkosh, Nebraska, Boring, Oregon, Why, Arizona, Why Not, Mississippi, Loafers Glory, North Carolina, Sweet Lips, Tennessee, Lonelyville, N.Y. (they need a little love), Do Stop, Kentucky and my personal favorite, Hopeulikit, Georgia.

Many candidates shy away from the major issues facing this country, but not this Donald – The Donald.

1) I oppose taxation of children's Lemonade stands.

2) I support natural energy—solar power, wind power, and methane gas power from the dairy cattle in Texas. We will harvest this "natural gas" and ship it to states in need. (Share the wealth)

3) All people are welcome in America, as long as, they can pass the U.S. "litmus test." They have to be able to read the periodic table backwards and they have to know the atomic number of each chemical element. In addition, they have to agree to be a "test driver" for 1 year in a Google, self driving, (autonomous) vehicle, in order to earn money and pay taxes.

4) Social Security will be renamed "Social Insecurity."

5) Lastly, because most of those who currently represent us in Washington, don't get along very well, I will implement a new policy which states that "all of them," I repeat, "all of them" must attend a "playground" sensitivity training program. They will practice sharing the swings, slides and climbing equipment. Those who fail the course, will be ticketed at "speed traps" on their way home.

I will continue to unveil other, very important policies, in upcoming issues of my Senior Citizens newsletter.

Thank you for your support,

      Pappy Donald (The Real Deal)
      VOTE FOR ME! No good reason, just askin' 

VOLUME 1

CHAPTER 2

The Donald Campaign Message

The Example

12/06/2015

Dear Staffee,

That's the familiar form of staff. It shows love, devotion, humility and, and quite frankly, it gives a big bear hug to each of you without being present. It also leads me into some of my recent findings on political persuasion and what this country is lacking today.

First; If you haven't noticed recently, there seem to be a lot of people that are watching the example of our politicians in Washington. (See my diatribe from last week regarding their lack of "friendliness" toward each other.) People are not getting along very well. When kids grow up in this world they often look up to other people, whether it's their parents, older siblings, aunts, uncles or someone they admire and want to emulate. The problem is, it's getting harder to find anyone to admire.

Athlete's?   that doesn't work.   Their too busy getting overpaid. Some are using what we'll call "not so good stuff" to enhance performance. Take a look at our track stars, "Tour de France" bicyclists, baseball players, football players, weight lifting, you bet. I haven't heard of problems in ballet yet but, ...?   So let's go to business leaders. Heard about any political contribution problems lately?   Any automobile manufacturers with mileage inflation problems? Parents must be watching a lot of C-Span lately, because they disagree with each other to the point that they won't share cell phones, drink out of the same cup and just don't live at the same address anymore. How about movie stars? oops! that one isn't worth wasting typing space over. Politicians? A Deseret News article dated Jan 23rd, 2014 lists 20 notable politicians convicted of crimes since 2000. What should we do? I'll list some antidotes to this mess next week.

Second, Debt!   How do we convince our best and brightest to balance their home budget when Washington, hasn't the faintest idea how to do it especially, if they want to get reelected in the next election.   We hurt feelings when we balance a budget. So, they say, let's just pass along the problem to the next administration or generation.   They actually, whisper this statement so that no one who votes for them is within hearing distance of their comment.

And a third national problem, that may eclipse all other major national issues for decades. Cereal. That's right, Cereal. Anyone notice lately that cereal, the national food of champions, think Wheaties, is now packaged in smaller boxes. Yes, the 24 ounce box you once loved, which cost about $2.00 is now a 13.2 ounce box for $3.29, on sale. Now, the manufactures didn't spring this one on us overnight. They followed the CIA formula. Be covert. Pretend that consumers are basically stupid, even though the number of educated citizens is on the increase in the U.S.

First, we'll make the box a little shorter, with fewer ounces. Then, we'll make the inner plastic bags with less tear material so the consumer can't rip the bag open without sending cereal into the stratosphere. Ah, next will make the box thinner. The consumer will never know that their entire hand now wraps around the whole box. Ounces, now 12.375. Cost, $3.49 but, with natural ingredients. Never mind that it's still oats and rice. That consumer couldn't tell the difference anyway at least, they feel healthy and their cholesterol is down a 1/4 of a point. At least Mikey doesn't care….see attached video!

Mikey Likes Life

https://www.youtube.com/watch?v=vYEXzx-TINc

About a year ago, I kidded a very important person in my life, that the day was coming when we would see a single serving size of cereal for $2.00. I thought this would happen in my lifetime. Blow me away! Two weeks ago, we saw cereal on the shelves, just a little over a single serving, two for $3.00. The manufactures are sneaky, kind of like the NSA, you get 2 for $3.00. A $1.50 a piece. Next time in, watch, single serving for $2.00. Holy Toledo! (Ever wonder where this term came from?) Speculation is; the heavy concentration of churches on Collingwood Boulevard.

Where is all of this leading to for "The Real Donald" campaign? Stay tuned next week for answers to these perplexing national issues. This Donald doesn't mind tackling the tough issues head-on.

May your week be filled with nothing but positive experiences. No Murphy's!

Donald

VOLUME 1

CHAPTER 3

The Donald Campaign Message

Citizens of Rome

12/13/2015

Citizens of Rome!

I can tell that my Presidential campaign is beginning to gain momentum mainly, because others in the race are so busy trying to pick on each other that they don't see me sneaking up from behind. In addition, they are not aware of the issues that really confront the great citizens of this country i.e. taxation of lemonade stands, social insecurity and the great American cereal Rip-off that they fail to address these issues in a timely manner.

The public, being keenly aware that the average size wallet, which used to have money in it, is now half the thickness it used to be because it now contains only "get out of jail, free cards" stored up from 1960's era Monopoly games. The citizens hold on to these cards, in hope, that after they have given 75% of their wages in taxes to the government that they can use the card when the IRS wants to send them away for not giving 80%. By the way, where do all of these taxes go anyway? When people, in this case Congress, can vote to give themselves a raise, whenever they choose and they are the ones allocating our tax money to a variety of causes, shouldn't we be a little suspect? Research shows that when a person receives free money, money they don't work for, they tend to use less discretion on how it is used and by the way, our current U.S. National Deficit is $18Trillion. which is 1000 X one Billion = 1 trillion. What does this look like?

Please take a look at this video. It will knock your "socks off" if, you had any to wear. The reason you're probably not wearing any socks is because the IRS took those also.

https://www.youtube.com/watch?v=iC6CgxuPBjs
**(NOTE: At the time of printing this video
was no longer available)**

I am considering Herb Bunk as my Vice Presidential running mate. More on him later!

Now, about the cereal issue:

Since you probably didn't have time to read the whole article, I'll summarize. "WE'RE PAYING MORE AND GETTING LESS."

My solution to these problems is simple: "We will praise the good and Fix the bad" What does that mean? Stay tuned for next weeks newsletter. I will clearly elaborate the meaning of this new banner, which will hang from the rooftops of all of our faithful citizens. We will also discuss a new problem that faces our nation, "What in the world is the Consumer Price Index?" and how come the politicians in Washington D.C. don't know either?

Let's run our chariots all the way to the end of this race!

The Real Donald speaks!

VOLUME 1

CHAPTER 4

The Donald Campaign Message

Contributions

12/27/2015

Dear Citizens, Countrymen, Countrywomen and anyone else interested in knowing why Pluto should still be considered a planet, in my humble opinion;

First, an update on the status of my financial contributions and the success of my campaign. While many of my colleagues and competitors in this Presidential campaign require large sums of money from their Political Action Committees (PACs) and Billionaire donations to survive the long, grueling months ahead, I can assure those who support me that my campaign will remain solvent from start to finish.

I will not require last minute donations from supporters and I will not go into debt, as many of those running for this esteemed office, have encountered in the last 10 elections. As a result, I will not be beholden to any PAC and I will not find myself in a position to give VIP appointments (i.e Ambassador to the Tibetan people in the Himilayas) to those who have given me a billion dollars.

The reason I have this distinct pleasure is that, so far, my total received revenue, which by the way is audited by the venerable (Deloitte, Touche and Tohmatsu Accounting firm) is $0.00 dollars. My total expenditures, to date, are $0.00.

Now, for the Real Donald speech of the week;
As I mentioned last week, a key to fixing this mess we are in nationally, is to be fiscally responsible. We can't continue to spend, spend, spend and then consider increasing taxes to our citizens. Here are some interesting facts for the American people to consider and our politicians to digest.

1) The federal tax code was 400 pages in 1913. In 2010 it was 70,000 pages.

2) The Bible has about 700,000 words. The number of words in the Federal Tax Code: 3,700,000.
My take on that: If God can say everything He needs to tell us in 700,000 words than why would it take 5 times that many words to tell us we basically work for the government. We need to simplify. By the way, who actually understands this code anyway? Any chance for a mistake to be made?

While we're talking about documents that govern our lives but, that no one understands, how about the Consumer Price Index. So, what is it and why does it matter? Well, here's how the gov't defines it: The *Consumer Price Index (CPI)* is a measure of the average change over time in the *prices* paid by urban *consumers* for a market basket of *consumer* goods and services.

Ok, that sounds pretty straight forward doesn't it? We should see from this definition why the cost of goods, we buy as consumers, go up or down (which never happens).

Question: What goods and services does the Consumer Price Index (CPI) cover?

Answer: The CPI represents all goods and services purchased for consumption by the reference population (Consumer Price Index for All Urban Consumers or Consumer Price Index for Urban Wage Earners and Clerical Workers). The Bureau of Labor Statistics (BLS) has classified all expenditure items into more than 200 categories, arranged into eight major groups. Major groups and examples of categories in each are as follows:

- FOOD AND BEVERAGES (breakfast cereal, milk, coffee, chicken, wine, full service meals and snacks);

- HOUSING (rent of primary residence, owners' equivalent rent, fuel oil, bedroom furniture);

- APPAREL (men's shirts and sweaters, women's dresses, jewelry);

- TRANSPORTATION (new vehicles, airline fares, gasoline, motor vehicle insurance);

•MEDICAL CARE (prescription drugs and medical supplies, physicians' services, eyeglasses and eye care, hospital services);

•RECREATION (televisions, cable television, pets and pet products, sports equipment, admissions);

•EDUCATION AND COMMUNICATION (college tuition, postage, telephone services, computer software and accessories);

•OTHER GOODS AND SERVICES (tobacco and smoking products, haircuts and other personal services, funeral expenses).

Also included within these major groups are various government-charged user fees, such as water and sewerage charges, auto registration fees, and vehicle tolls. The CPI also includes taxes, such as sales and excise taxes, that are directly associated with the prices of specific goods and services. However, the CPI excludes taxes, such as income and Social Security taxes, not directly associated with the purchase of consumer goods and services.

Here's my question: When a box of cereal, let's say Wheaties, costs $2.98 for 16 ounces (18.7 cents per ounce)in January, now in December, it costs $3.00 so the CPI says it was a marginal increase of .07% increase for the year. Not much, huh? BUT! The same box, is now only 14.2ounces or (21.1 cents per ounce) does the CPI calculate that difference? My guess is no. Many of these goods in the market basket probably change like that over time.

Gas has such large season swings that it tends to offset the increase in goods and make the whole basket look less expensive than it is. Well, my point is that the CPI is not on the radar for my opponents. Frankly, they don't consider it and better yet they don't care.

Second question: If this CPI only covers urban consumers, what happens to rural consumers? I guess they don't use any of the above products? or maybe, they just don't count! Jen and Mark, you're off the hook because you're not urban. Technically, Bountiful is not an urban area but it is considered an urban cluster so, I think mom and I, and Justin and Emily, Troy and Kelsi, and soon, Kelby and Mallory will be in an urban cluster or rural too. So, don't worry about inflation either, because it doesn't affect you either.

If you ask me, the following individuals should be in a Market Research Study. They should be included in a Focus Group and they should be asked questions about "What do you think about the CPI?"

You'll want to seen this one.

Art Linkletter KIDS SAY THE DARNDEST THINGS

https://www.youtube.com/watch?v=EBMOhM31EyM

Well, where does all this lead me in the "Real Donald" campaign? Simply said: The other candidates are barking up the wrong tree! **They** are addressing the wrong issues. The issues I have listed each week, are the issues most voters are looking to us, as candidates, for answers.

The banner that is unfurled, should include the issues, I have listed.

As a concluding remark for this week. Why does everyone keep picking on Pluto. First, they say it is a planet, then they say it isn't. Here's why:

This group decided that **Pluto** was **not** really a **planet** because of its size and location in space. So **Pluto** and objects like it are now called dwarf **planets**. **Pluto** is also called a plutoid. A plutoid is a dwarf **planet** that is farther out in space than the **planet** Neptune.

Did they just discover that Pluto was small? I thought they knew this decades ago. Did they just discover that Pluto is way out there? Past Neptune? I thought they knew this too. Are these scientists just discovering science?
I do have to admit that I think it is nice that Pluto is now called a plutoid. That name has a "catchy" ring to it.

In my Presidency, Pluto will be returned to its rightful status as a planet. Maybe, I'll also require those choosing to become citizens of the USA to define plutoid. Maybe, anyone who wants to vote in the upcoming election should be required to define plutoid?
And, besides that, Disney named one of their favorite dog characters after the planet Pluto. What other planet in our system has that distinction.

Vote: The Real Donald in 2016, it will make you happy!

Donald!

VOLUME 1

CHAPTER 5

The Donald Campaign Message

A New Year

01/02/2016

Welcome to 2016- the year of the New President!

Who will it be? I am sure you are asking yourself that very question, right now. Will it be someone you choose or will it be someone the "others choose?" Who are the "others?" They are the ones that spend no time researching the candidates, in fact, they don't even care to know what the platform is for the candidate they will vote for in the election. They just vote for gender or for someone who promises to give them phones or someone who "best of all" says one thing and does another, knowingly.

Well, next week, at the request of my supporters, I will address some non-economic issues that face our nation. But tonight, I am changing course for one week, to do what my esteemed colleagues will not do and that is to address religion and spiritual goals for the year.

As we were returning home from Muleshoe, Mom, Cody and I read the first lesson for Gospel Doctrine. The Book of Mormon is the 'keystone" of our religion. Now, this is not new to most of us but, there were quotes that I thought were pertinent to making 2016 a good, better, maybe perfect year for our families. We know the Book of Mormon was written for our time so what does it tell us? What conditions did Moroni foresee would exist in the world when the BOM was again brought forth?

"The power of God shall be denied" (verse 28) Is this true today? We had an active discussion in the car and each of us enumerated ways God is denied His rightful place in our world. It's interesting to note that in the movie, "Unbroken" the crux of the movie is on Zamperini's extraordinary life and survival during wartime. What Hollywood didn't show, was that the Lord intervened in his life when he was at, perhaps the worst time of his life, after the war.

"There shall be great pollutions upon the face of the earth." (verse 31). We discussed whether this was literal pollution or a pollution of spirit among today's people. Cody said one of his professor's at BYU stated, in many cases, these types of verses refer to both.

People will "lift themselves up in the pride of their hearts" (verse 36). Is this apparent today? What does entitlement mean today?

People will "love money...more than they will love the poor and the needy" (verse 37) That's funny! Don't we see more and more, that every decision that is made, in corporate America, and in local America, is all about money? Why do they start college games at 9:00 pm at night? Who really comprises the poor and needy?

People will be "ashamed to take upon themselves the name of Christ." Do we find as Elder Perry stated, "the minority masquerading as the majority" when it comes to taking down nativity scenes in towns, making sure we say Happy Holidays instead of Merry Christmas because we don't want to offend people on Christ's Birthday. For Heaven's Sake, whose birthday is it anyway, Happy Holidays? If they don't like us saying Merry Christmas, then they don't have to celebrate the 25th. Maybe, these people can celebrate someone else's birthday in June, if they like.

As I stated, each of the major writers of the BOM testified that he wrote for future generations. ...If they saw our day and chose those things which would be of greatest worth to us, is not that how we should study the Book of Mormon? We should constantly ask, ourselves, "Why did the Lord inspire Mormon or Moroni or Alma to include that in his record?

Now for goals: Mom and I have found through the years that if, in January, we set spiritual goals, family goals, financial goals, business or work goals and personal goals (e.g.) reading a book we've wanted to read or exercise etc., we do better. For us these goals are simple, just something we want to accomplish that year. In most years, we have progressed far more than in years we haven't written down these goals.

We don't try to get to elaborate or write too many goals under each category but, even one goal makes you feel a sense of accomplishment, if you achieve it, at the end of the year. You might try it, if you aren't already.

And finally, attached is a blank copy of our Budget Tracker. You may need to eliminate certain rows that don't fit your specific needs. Our tracker has become quite lengthy through the years because of the size of our family. Obviously, mortgage can change to rent for some of you. I then put in the formulas to add rows left to right or top to bottom. The top section is basic, monthly costs, whereas the bottom third of the page are expenses that happen occasionally. It's interesting that every financial planner told us that 90% of people don't keep track of their monthly/yearly expenses so they don't really know how much they spend per month or what they spend it on. This may be a good, simple document to start a budget and tracking your expenses. I'm sure there are other good documents but this one has worked for us.

Well, my fellow lemonade drinkers, all is well in Zion! Have a fun week and keep your chin up!

Love and vote, Donald 

VOLUME 1

CHAPTER 6

The Donald Campaign Message

Where's the Beef?

01/10/2016

"Where's the Beef?" Watch this!
https://www.youtube.com/watch?v=Ug75diEyiA0

All of the other candidates running this year, for any party, have a lot of "bun" but no beef!

That's right, very little substance. Why? Because they forget that the great citizens of America always ask the same questions each Presidential cycle but, the candidates never really give a full, direct answer. For example: when Bernie Sanders is asked if he is a socialist? Here's his response: Appearing on NBC's Meet the Press, Sanders engaged with host Chuck Todd in a easy back-and-forth regarding his brand of socialism.

"Alright," began Todd, "You joked about the idea when people call you a socialist, you say, 'Yes, I'm going to make everybody wear the same color pajamas.'"

"Especially you," replied Sanders.

"Especially me?" asked the host.

"I have a pair of pajamas just for you," said the candidate.

Now, my take on this is that "I like to have people wearing different pajama's." I don't think our Founding Fathers or the Constitution ever intended for us all to wear the same pajama's. After all some like bears and some like turtles.

One of the other major issues in this election is Terrorism. Ever heard of that topic in the newspapers, on radio, or the T.V. lately? What the other candidates don't understand is that religion has been a "bone of contention" for people for about a billion years. Ever heard of the Crusades? Seems people don't like other people who are not the same religion even though, most of the people will tell you that their religion tells them to "love each other" and "forgive each other" and "turn the other cheek." Too much bun, not enough beef!

I have a simple answer, everyone that wants to be a terrorist has to sit in the same room with other people they don't like and watch "Lion King" together. Half way through, they will all stand, join hands and sing "Hakuna Matata" several hundred times until they all want to hug each other and never have a "disposition to do evil." Look it works, just watch!

https://www.youtube.com/watch?v=xB5ceAruYrl
NOTE: At the time of publishing, this video was no longer available.

And finally, for this week, y'all know we went to the great state of Texas between Christmas and New Years. Well, we got stranded in a snow storm in Melrose, New Mexico. We, along with 53 other people, either slept in a convenience store, on the floor, with no heat or lights, or in our cars in the parking lot overnight. Now, that may sound bad but, it wasn't half bad. The problem was, the next day we had to deal with the local highway patrol officer who also spent the night, and who waited for some of us to finally gather everyone together and decide we would get out of Dodge. After he heard me say, "We're going" he said, "me too." We also had the privilege of dealing with a rear wheel drive plow, with bad passenger tires who got stuck, that's right stuck, not once, but twice trying to plow the snow. Guess who got the plow unstuck? Yes, indeed y'all, it was the 15 men and boys from the convenience store with shovels!!!!!!! It doesn't end there. Once we got the plow unstuck, he drove away, never to be seen again. Now there's government at its best.

Then, after we set up a caravan of cars and trucks to forge ahead for 30 minutes to Clovis, we first ran into the Highway Patrolman, who after we got him through the snow, went out in front for a while until, a herd of cows, that broke out of a fence, ran down the highway and we find this fine officer herding cows in his patrol car down the highway. He honked, they ran, but not in the direction he wanted them to.

Here's the clincher. Once through Clovis, on our way to Muleshoe, we encounter, a pickup towing a camper trailer jackknifed in the middle of the road. Not to worry, a 6000 pound Farm Tractor comes to the rescue and promptly gets stuck in a drift. Now the entire road is blocked and 40 mile an hour winds are blowing drifts around these 2 vehicles. Again, not to worry! The town sends out a grader but what's this, the grader can't push the snow, it's too deep. So the driver decides to turn around, go back to town and get a front loader. In the meantime, a massive Army vehicle from Fort Cannon comes to tow the Farm Tractor out of the way but, what's this, he can't get his vehicle to the tractor because the snow is too deep so, he turns around and goes back to town. Thirty minutes later, a front loader starts back to the blocked road but, by now, the police tell him to go back to town and come the next morning.

By now, you get my drift—-no pun intended! Gov't doesn't work very well and heaven forbid if we have an emergency. Better to go to the funeral parlor and pick out your coffin.

As President, I intend to fix this by giving every emergency vehicle a can, a long string and an edict to call each other and coordinate their matchbox trucks at the same time.

To prepare you for next week, watch this:

Sonny & Cher The Beat Goes On

https://www.youtube.com/watch?v=umrp1tIBY8Q

Yes, "The beat Goes On"

Vote The Real Donald to Save Our Country 

VOLUME 1

CHAPTER 7

The Donald Campaign Message

What Future?

01/17/2016

To anyone who cares, would like to care or may care in the future,

Last week I addressed some of the new concerns we face as a nation. Specifically, who do we turn to when we, as a people, need help? The old days are gone! Yep, Sayonara, Adios, Ciao, Au reveoir, Ahn youn hee ka se yo, arrivederci, bi xatre te, da svidaniya, ha det or my personal favorite——————See Ya Pal!

It use to be you could turn to almost anyone, to get directions when you were lost, when you ran out of gas, couldn't find something in a store, or were caught in a snowstorm in Melrose, New Mexico. Well, that ain't going to happen today. First of all, if you go into a service station and say I'm lost, can you help me get to________ (fill in the blank), the attendant doesn't speak your language (probably one of the above languages), he looks at you like you just escaped from one of the pens at the Hogle Zoo, or he thinks you can just use your GPS in the car. Guess what? A 1991 Nissan Sentra, by the name of Rambo, doesn't, I repeat, doesn't have GPS. As a matter of fact, my campaign vehicle, which you've already seen in prior newsletters, will never have GPS. I don't want to taint my vehicle. I want to get to those little towns on my own, with a map, and occasionally with the help of someone WHO CARES! Most people can't help you get where you want to go because they don't know how to get there either. Why? They don't know how to read a map or they can't speak your language or they just escaped from a pen at the Hogle Zoo!

What about if you run out of gas? Better arm yourself with a howitzer because no one will stop, you don't know which pen at the zoo they escaped from or they drive an electric car and don't know what gas is anyway. Why they say, do you need gas, as they drive away. Heaven forbid, if you ask for help to find something in a store. First the person growls at you, second they tell you they aren't paid enough (minimum wage of $15 an hour) or they really don't know where it is in the store either. The stores turn over employees ever 7 and a half seconds.
Yes, we are a nation in trouble! Oh, we got trouble. Just watch.........

The Music Man "Ya Got Trouble"

https://www.youtube.com/watch?v=Ll_Oe-jtgdI

Yes, we are at the tipping point, just like Aldous Huxley suggests in his book "Brave New World." Although the novel is set in the future it deals with contemporary issues of the early 20th century. An early trip to the United States gave Brave New World much of its character. Not only was Huxley outraged by the culture of youth, commercial cheeriness and sexual promiscuity, and the inward-looking nature of many Americans, he had also found the book My Life and Work by Henry Ford on the boat to America, and he saw the book's principles applied in everything he encountered after leaving San Francisco.[16]

Others running for President in 2016, have missed the boat. They think everything is Hunky Dorey! Why should we talk to each other? Why should we care about others? Why should we help others get out of the convenience store in Melrose, Texas.   Let's let the government do it. After all, they already provide us with Medicare, Medicaid, free cell phones, Social Insecurity, and a dozen other programs so, we don't have to work the rest of our lives. Put us in the pens, and tell us when the "food is in the trough" and we'll come eat.

Well, I have a solution. It's called the Marshmellow Test, or the Delayed Gratification Test. Everyone in America has been trained to "want everything, now. Right Now! And by the way, I want it my way–who cares about others!

Here's the test……

The Stanford marshmallow experiment[1] was a series of studies on delayed gratification in the late 1960s and early 1970s led by psychologist Walter Mischel, then a professor at Stanford University.

The Stanford marshmallow experiment[1] was a series of studies on delayed gratification in the late 1960s and early 1970s led by psychologist Walter Mischel, then a professor at Stanford University. In these studies, a child was offered a choice between one small reward provided immediately or two small rewards if they waited for a short period, approximately 15 minutes, during which the tester left the room and then returned. (The reward was sometimes a marshmallow, but often a cookie or a pretzel.) In follow-up studies, the researchers found that children who were able to wait longer for the preferred rewards tended to have better life outcomes, as measured by SAT scores,[2] educational attainment,[3] body mass index (BMI),[4] and other life measures.[5]

Here's what the test looks like with kids,

https://www.youtube.com/watch?v=0mWc1Y2dpmY

NOTE: At the time of publishing, the video was no longer available.

So, there you go. Adults act a lot like kids! We want our marshmallow now. We need a paradigm shift. After all, anyone who's going to provide a "better life outcome" by serving marshmallows is on to something.   Let's talk about that next week

Vote for the Real Donald   Marshmallows for everyone

VOLUME 1

CHAPTER 8

The Donald Campaign Message

Polling

01/24/2016

Poll: Public doubts Washington's problem-solving ability—
Deseret News Sunday, January 24th, 2016

"As the first voting nears in the presidential race, most Americans have little to no confidence in the federal government to confront what they see as the country's most important priorities, according to a national survey." This poll, conducted in December, found more than 6 in 10 respondents expressed only slight confidence—or none at all—that the federal government can make progress on the problems facing the nation in 2016."

Now for my question. How is this any different than the sentiments the American public felt in 2012, the last presidential year or what about the 1960 campaign or 1972? Yep, the answer to that quiz question is D., all of the above. In other words, these are the same doubts we, as Americans have had for the last 50 years, at least. Here are, I believe, some of the reasons.

1) "Mia Love, Representative from the Utah Congress wants to crack down on Congress dumping controversial legislation into unrelated, must-pass bills in the middle of the night. She has introduced a measure to limit bills in Congress to one subject at a time. It would prevent lawmakers from bundling things together or folding legislation into large appropriations bills. " NOW THIS IS NOVEL "Each bill would rise and fall on its own merits. Members of both parties have made a habit of passing complex, thousand-page bills without hearings, amendments or debate," Love said. That process and the collusion that goes with it are why we a $18 trillion in debt and why the American people have lost trust in elected officials." By the way, good for Mia Love.

Yes, this indeed used to be and probably still is called "Earmark's" or "Pork Barrel Spending."

Ok, so think of this. A thousand page bill, which by the way is probably the shortest of the bills, come on, who is going to read it? The running average number of bills passed each year by Congress is 758. That's 758,000 pages!

No way, you say!

Solution: Yep, As President, I would support Mia's proposal. It is better. One bill, one subject pass it or not! No back-room deals.   I bet George Washington, Benjamin Franklin, Thomas Jefferson and even Paul Revere would support me.

"One if by land, and two if by sea!" Shine the lights on this baby.

2) Why else do American's feel the government can't solve the IMPORTANT issues?

Well, here are a couple of thoughts from noted men in history:

"In my many years I have come to a conclusion that one useless man is a shame, two is a law firm, and three or more is a congress."
   JOHN ADAMS, second US president

"Suppose you were an idiot, and suppose you were a member of Congress; but I repeat myself."
   Mark Twain

or here's one that reminds me of Justin's dialogue in "Homeowners Political Plight."

"Congress is so strange. A man gets up to speak and says nothing. Nobody listens—-and then everybody disagrees." Boris Marshalov (not sure who he is but he has it right)

Is there any wonder why the American people are fed Up? It may be time for a second American Revolution. Let's get a President and a Congress who want to get things done. Identify each problem, of which, there are now 62 billion 372 million on and on and on that need to be addressed because our Congress has been so inept and they just want to sit and "eat pork barrel" sandwiches.

3) Any President who is elected today, has to have a sense of humor because he/she is basically, joining the circus. Think, Hogle Zoo1

Here's one who knew how to do it:

The Best of Ronald Reagan

https://www.youtube.com/watch?v=yVYtIdUcYqY

I like this approach else, why would I be doing what I am doing right now. Stay tune for next week!

Vote the real Donald! 

VOLUME 1

CHAPTER 9

The Donald Campaign Message

Here We Go Again

01/31/2016

Well, here we go folks. The Iowa Caucus is this week and the New Hampshire Primary is close behind. All of the candidates are now worried because "The Real Donald" campaign has gained so much momentum in such a short time. In fact newspaper headlines describe the disarray the other campaign's face in realizing the trouble they may encounter. "Feuds flare up as clock ticks down toward caucuses in Iowa." Deseret News, January 31, 2016.

It's going go be a real horse race to the finish.

Just watch:

NOTE: At the time of publishing this video was no longer available.

Did you see all of my opponents riding those horses. Are you worried about them? Probably, because they have a few bumps and bruises from falling off those thoroughbreds.

Soon, I'll be riding circles around them;

Trick Horseback Riders

*https://www.**youtube**.com/watch?v=EgwJyQ-YdJc*

It's time for this campaign to take on a "Theme Song" so, here's mine:

Mr. Ed - Intro (Opening Theme)

https://www.youtube.com/watch?v=y_PZPpWTRTU

Now is the time to put all of these great ideas from the last 3 months together to push this campaign over the top. The American people want to see someone who can create jobs. Not that everyone wants to work but, I would promote factories in the U.S. to build iwheelchairs and icouches. I would likely call them zwheelchairs and zcouches because the poor letter "Z" always gets left in the dark. Last in the alphabet, hardly any words start with Z and most people, who would buy and race these wheelchairs and lie on the couches that move from the family room to the kitchen, would probably be catching up on their Zzzzzz's.

Well, I definitely want people to get back to work. Such talent out there that's untapped. We want citizens that know how to keep up with technology and more importantly, they find solutions to problems and "think on their feet."

Here's a couple that know how to do it right:

https://www.youtube.com/watch?v=8NPzLBSBzPl
NOTE: At the time of publishing this video was no longer available.

Remember, Vote The Real Donald, the one who knows how to ride the horse to the end of the race.

VOLUME 1

CHAPTER 10

The Donald Campaign Message

Just Made It

02/07/2016

Whew!

We just made it through the Iowa Caucus and now we're on our way to winning New Hampshire this week. As usual, it will require our greatest effort to convince the "Granite State" citizens that our campaign supports their "Live free or Die" motto, as much as, we support corn syrup subsidies in Iowa. In January 1776 it became the first of the British North American colonies to establish a government independent of Great Britain's authority and it was the first to establish its own state constitution.

I'm pretty sure this state is "wrapped up" (no pun intended) because they have "no sales tax" which means they'll love my "no new taxes" sandwich which I will provide while visiting each city in the state.

Basically, the sandwich will consist of 2 pieces of bread, hardened like granite, no meat (we don't want their cholesterol to go up), 2 pickles, 1 leaf of "dyed, blue lettuce to represent their state flag, and mustard on the bread that states, "Live free or die." I already did a "feasibility study" in the state. Two people agreed it was the worse tasting sandwich they have ever eaten but, it was perfect because it reminded them of how gov't is run. Blah! Blah! Blah! It was a hit!

I'm fully confident that they will eagerly accept my proposal for "Curbs on funding from traffic tickets." The following article in the Deseret News explains my rationale,

SALT LAKE CITY — A state lawmaker says the small Box Elder County town of Mantua is a speed trap.

Sen. Lyle Hillyard, R-Logan, said one-third of the town's budget is supported by traffic ticket revenue.

"This is the only place I get complaints about in my district," he told the Senate Transportation and Public Utilities and Technology Committee on Monday.

Hillyard is sponsoring SB100, which would cap the amount of revenue a municipality can collect from traffic tickets at 25 percent of its budget. The committee sent the bill to the full Senate with a unanimous recommendation.

Mantua is a town of 687 residents, according to the 2010 census. The town is not specifically listed in the proposed legislation, but Hillyard says he is sponsoring the bill because he's had many constituents complain about getting tickets there.

Other states have imposed similar revenue caps, he said, including Virginia, Missouri, Oklahoma and Florida.

While there has historically been many fatal car crashes in Sardine Canyon, Hillyard said the concrete barriers that now divide the highway have increased safety in the canyon and strict policing is not as needed as it once was.

Mantua Mayor and Police Chief Mike Johnson says the improved safety in the canyon has nothing to do with the barriers.

"In all the time I spent with the highway patrol, I never saw those barriers on the highway stop any accidents or do away with fatal accidents," he said.

Johnson said police recently ticketed someone for going 108 mph in a 60 mph zone, and that there are frequently cars traveling more than 90 mph there.

Four DUI arrests since Dec. 1, he said, has made the area safer for both Mantua residents and Hillyard's constituents in Logan.

"I think that we're sending a message and getting people to slow down," Johnson said.

Johnson is Mantua's one full-time police officer, and there are three additional part-time officers.

To clear up misconceptions, Mantua financial analyst Lorrie Herd presented the actual revenue generated by the tickets.

Herd said 42 to 43 percent of the revenue goes back to the state. Last year, that left the town with $246,000. The cost of funding the police department and court system takes roughly $229,000 a year, leaving the town with $17,000.

This year, revenue from July 1 through Dec. 31 leaves the town with a net of $23,000, she said. After around $14,000 is taken out to help fund the fire department, the town will have gained a net of approximately $9,000.

If Hillyard's bill passes, Herd says Mantua will have a budget shortfall of more than $100,000.

Anyone who wants to Live free or die, can't stand traffic tickets!

SCORE:The Real Donald ..2 other candidates 0.

Now the other advantage "The Real Donald" and the "The Real First Lady" have is that we have lived in New England. We know that people there are down to earth. They don't like to mess around. They have everything under control. Just watch: The Shemp vs an ironing board for 1 minute 29 seconds.

The Three Stooges: Shemp VS an Ironing board. IN COLOR

https://www.youtube.com/watch?v=4ZG6l_wF4e0

So, there you have it. New Hampshire is a slam dunk.
Once they see this video and I explain how I would get
things done in Washington, well, it's "ALL ABOARD" to
the Nations Capital.

SCORE: The Real Donald..3 other candidates).

Wish me well this week or Wish me Happy Birthday or
Wish me to go away.

It's the Bowl of Super alias The Real Donald   

VOLUME 1

CHAPTER 11

The Donald Campaign Message

Continue on Our Way

02/14/2016

Now that the New Hampshire primary is behind us and New England is buried in 4 feet of snow and temp's could feel as low as minus 35, it's time to move on to the south and west.

Thanks to all of my New Hampshire supporters who braved the cold, waited until the last minute to make a decision on who to vote for, decided to be neither republican or democrat and basically, took the day off to go skiing. Way to Go!

We continue on our way to Bictory. (That's Bickering, as in debates, and Victory, as in, Look out for my dust.)
In Nevada and South Carolina, I intend to remind the voters-No Campaign-No Gain! Wanta know why?

Just watch:

NOTE: At the time of publishing this video was no longer available.

Now if that doesn't make you want to loose weight, vote or just get sick to your stomach, you're not human. Vote for me anyway!

This trip to the south and west is going to require a lot of patience and persistence. We will have to travel long distances to canvas these states and help the voters know that "The Real Donald" is coming to the rescue:

Lone Ranger Opening Theme

https://www.youtube.com/watch?v=QCO6smQrjJ8

Of course, they will have to remember that my campaign vehicle has some limitations, remember?

Hey Mark, where's my back-up cow? This mare is looking tired. She's already seen thousands of miles and every time I say "Hi Ho Silver" she just ignores me.

Maybe, we need a little Carpool Karoke to perk her up?

Adele Carpool Karaoke: Coming Wednesday

https://www.youtube.com/watch?v=O6REBmZ0NDY

I think this mare will giddy-up after hearing that inspiring music. Whatcha think?

I have heard that the voters in Nevada are distraught with the options for the presidency this year. They are looking for someone with more courage to take on our enemies in the world. Someone, who has the heart to care about our local citizens in America and someone, with the brains to figure out E=MCsquared. I have a couple of ideas for them:

Judy Garland - Follow the yellow brick road

https://www.youtube.com/watch?v=RmqRx3ypWwU

Mew World Order: Siberian City Backs Cat for Mayor
by The Associated Press

BARNAUL, Russia — Tired of the dog-eat-dog politics in their Russian city, the residents of Barnaul say they want a cat to be their next mayor.

The Siberian city of 650,000 people, which lies 1,800 miles east of Moscow, is to get a new mayor next week when a commission comprising the city council and the regional governor choose from among six candidates.:

But none of the six appear to spark much affection among Barnaul's residents. An informal online poll asking residents to express their preferences among the six and a Siamese cat named Barsik showed the feline nabbing more than 90 percent of the vote.

Barsik has attracted much amused attention in the Russian news media. Still, some local politicians understand there's a more serious message coming from the people of Barnaul, which like many Russian cities has been riddled with alleged corruption.

"Through the image of Barsik the cat, our people are sending definite wishes to the future head of Barnaul," says regional Gov. Alexander Karlin.

The Associated Press
Topics World
First Published Dec 19 2015, 8:05 pm ET

We will definitely need Justin's help to translate, if the Cat decides to run for president. He'll have to translate for the cat, all of the slanderous statements made against him, from the other candidates who worry he may win. ME? I'm not worried if a cat wins, I'll just go to work for Ralston-Purina and make a mint selling wholesome cat chow.

Well, there you have it folks.

One parting message: "I have wondered at times what the Ten Commandments would have looked like if Moses had run them through the US Congress. Ronald Reagan

I guess, I wonder the same thing?

Vote the Real Donald 

VOLUME 1

CHAPTER 12

The Donald Campaign Message

How About Them Broncos!

02/21/2016

The title of my campaign message this week sounds a little like a play in the Super Bowl, doesn't it? And by the way, how bout' them Broncos! Just lovin' that score. If they can win so, can the "Real Donald."

Yep, it's four states down and 46 to go before we know the winner of the 2016 presidential race. South Carolina and Nevada were good to us. I'm pretty sure I picked up a half of a delegate in each state. That should produce a whole, unless the government has found a way to tax delegates too and then I might only end up with 2/3 of a delegate. Either way, it exceeds expectations! We're on a roll.

Speaking of rolls! Notice how people just keep fighting around the world? Everyone wants to chime in, According to the U.N. there are 10 major wars going on around the world today with 32 intrastate wars. A President has to have a plan. So,here's my plan:

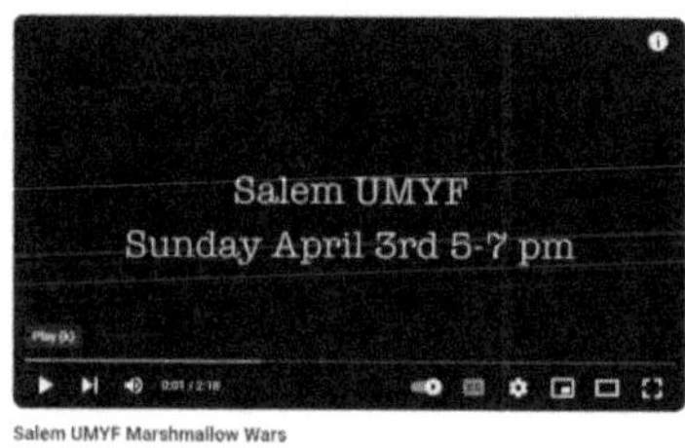

Salem UMYF Marshmallow Wars

https://www.youtube.com/watch?v=QETGfVOi1mA

Put all of the leaders of these countries in a gym and let them have 250 marshmallows. The first person knocked out with a marshmallow is out of the war. This continues until a winner has taken over all of the territory of the losing leader. But, you ask, what happens if no one is knocked out by a flying marshmallow? Ah, they all return home and a contract is signed that they cannot war with each other until everyone on earth returns to being a farmer and likes beats. Humm! I wonder how long that will be?

Farmer? That reminds me, we have a travesty in America. We need more people to return to their roots, farming. Hundreds of acres of farmland. No more cry babies! Oh, I hurt my toe, I stumbled on the carpet. I'm laid up for weeks. My pinkie finger hurts, I had to lift up a can of soup. Laid up for months. That's what we hear, all of the whiners! Let's take care of that, shall we?

https://www.youtube.com/watch?v=H7yZdOl_e_c

NOTE: At the time of publishing this video was no longer available

Paul Harvey has it right. We need the people who run this country to care about the country, the people who live in it and, about the future of America. All we have in Washington now, is the whiners. Why? because they have no "common sense," which is defined as "sound judgement in practical matters." Sound judgement? The politicians in Washington think this has something to do physic's, like giving an opinion about sound waves. And every time they have or give an opinion, they think they need to "write a bill" or "make a law." Yep, let's make a new law that restricts how much "common sense" people can have. Practical matters? we better write a bill limiting the use of common sense in practical matters. We wouldn't want a country full of people that make good decisions, just because it is the right thing to do, do we? After all, "according to a new estimate, Congress has had a full work week just 14 percent of the time since 1978." I mean, "Congress said they planned to address an important report next week because it's already Tuesday." Jimmy Kimmel

I guess it just goes to show, "You can lead a man to Congress, but you can't make him think." Milton Berle
Lest we think, it's just our politicians, how about this; "if the cash you doled out for a Las Vegas cab ride hurt your wallet, it's not all in you head--auditors in Nevada (by the way, the state, where they just voted for a woman, who I won't name, who received $3.15 million from Wall Street businesses for speeches given in 2013, according to CNN) also think taxi rates are outrageous. Las Vegas area cabs are overcharging customers to the tune of $47 million a year." Deseret News

That makes me wonder? Do you remember when gas prices were high and going up? Restaurants, airlines and trucking services charged an excise tax on deliveries of food, meals and airline tickets. WHY? because they said gas cost them so much. Now that gas is below $2.00, did these restaurants, airlines or trucking companies give that money back to the customers? Oh! they forgot. I'm sure it's coming next week.

Give us an honest farmer. How about an honest Native American. We kicked them off of their land and gave them some sub-par desert property.
We need housewives, mothers, firemen, pilots and just, plain good people to run our country. I'm thinking that anyone who attended this show in 1964 is probably a prime candidate for a political office.

The Beatles on the Ed Sullivan Show

https://www.youtube.com/watch?v=JC0MEF6d1eU

If you can scream like that, you should be able to be heard from the floor of the chamber. Besides, you don't have to say much of importance and you only have to show up on Mondays and Tuesdays.

Carry on till tomorrow!

The Real Donald

VOLUME 1

CHAPTER 13

The Donald Campaign Message

Hold On

02/28/2016

As I continue down this campaign trail, I recognize that the best part of walking or (riding in my Rambo chariot) is that I can meet so many cool people and I can observe so many neat places in life. So, today I share with you some of life's learning's that make me not only, a better candidate but, a better person!   Here we go…………….Hold on!

*https://www.youtube.com/watch?v=Q5mHPo2yDG8*NOTE: At the time of publishing this video was no longer available

Now that I have your attention (and by the way, Jeff Gordon should have been drinking lemonade from one of the children's stands in his neighborhood instead of Pepsi if he supported local business) we can look at some of the other great people out there who have practical ideas for families in our country.

What Practical Life Skills/Values Are You Going To Teach Your Children?
by Ann Simpson

It's important that we teach our children practical life skills—skills that teach them how to survive in society—how to thrive in society. These practical life skills can be divided into at least six categories and the skills that fall within each category are many, varied and probably endless. The question then arises as to which life skills you value and which life skills you and your spouse want to teach to your children. I'd like to share with you what I am teaching my children—

Communication skills. It is absolutely critical that people learn how to effectively communicate with one another, both verbally and through the written word. I'm teaching my kids the following—

* Be truthful—your word means everything
* Speak kindly—don't be hurtful with the words you use
* Say please, thank you, no thank you, etc. People appreciate manners
* Eye contact is very important
* As important as your words are, your actions are even more important

- When in doubt, ask questions
- Being able to organize and write your thoughts down on paper is important
- Realize that what you write may be read by many people–unintended readers as well as intended readers
- Be very careful what you write/post on social network sites
- Never, ever, ever use your communication skills to bully or make fun of anyone

A similar important skill set is the formation and maintenance of relationships. The ability to form and maintain relationships affects every aspect of our lives. Relationship beliefs and skills that I want my children to master include–

- Treat others as you would like to be treated yourself
- Do not confuse kindness for weakness. Recognize and value kindness
- It's important to be reliable
- There is no such thing as being too polite, too kind, or too reliable
- Value other people's time
- Friends come and go–but your family is forever
- Empathy–it's very important
- It is better to love and to be hurt, than never to love at all (I believe Shakespeare said it so much better!)
- You love people for their faults as well as their strengths
- It's important to treat animals kindly
- Treat other people's property with respect
- As important as your words are, actions are even more important (so important, it's mentioned more than once)
- Be kind to those that love you
- You have instincts for a reason. If something or someone doesn't feel right, trust yourself
- Compromise is important
- You don't always have to be right
- It really is more fun to give than to receive

- Financial skills are extremely important as money is a necessary part of life. The repercussions of not having these skills can be devastating. Financial skills that I want my children to learn include–
- Understand the value of money
- Know how to budget and live within your budget
- Know how to make money through investment vehicles such as money market accounts, 401Ks, stock options, etc., and know how to purchase/invest in these vehicles
- The concept of compound interest
- If an investment opportunity looks too good to be true, then it probably is
- The importance of a FICO score
- The importance and pitfalls of credit
- Know how to make a dollar go a long way

- Day to day living skills/concepts are certainly important and should not be undervalued. Every day living skills/concepts that I want my children to master include–
- Know your way around a computer–know how to fix things–know how to use programs
- Understand that Math and Science are extremely important
- History is not dull. You really can learn from other's mistakes and triumphs
- Know how to swim
- Know how to maintain a vehicle so you don't run out of oil and so your windshield wipers always work
- Be able to change a tire
- If you make something from scratch it gives you a personal sense of accomplishment
- One man's trash is another's treasure
- Know how to do the wash, hem your pants, sew on buttons, and iron a garment

- Know how to make healthy food
- Know how to read a label
- Know how to make a dollar go a long way (also a financial skill)

Philosophical lessons are very important and can have an effect on one's happiness. I want my children to understand the following–
Thoughts are very powerful
Enjoy what you have
Always do your best. Realize your best may change from day to day
It's ok to be wrong–in fact, that's how we learn
If something looks too good to be true, it probably is (again, important enough to be listed more than once)
Value and nurture your creativity
Value and nurture your own quiet times. Take time to rejuvenate
Religious/Spiritual Lessons–these are very important, very personal and very family driven lessons. My children do have a foundation. They have their beliefs. One of my children recently commented that I teach by example. She had no idea what a wonderful compliment that was!

We do teach by example…as well as in lesson form. And it's our responsibility to make sure our children possess the skills necessary to survive — even to thrive in the real world.

So, the question is, what do you and your spouse want to teach your children?

See what I mean? So much to learn from others if, we have an open mind.

Of course the problem is most candidates running for office have forgotten how to be practical.

Take a listen to this: Paul Harvey says it like no other;

www.npr.org/.../the-rest-of-the-story-paul–harvey-conservative-talk

Now that's what I've learned this week and that should make you want to get out and vote or, at least ask a bunch of good questions to those who are running for office. Go ask those good questions!

Love, the "REAL DONALD" vote, vote, vote..

VOLUME 1

CHAPTER 14

The Donald Campaign Message

Milestone

03/06/2016

Yes campaign staff, we have reached a milestone for the Presidential Election of 2016. The state caucuses and primaries are coming and going faster than bees around a hive. The number of "Real Donald" supporters just keeps growing by quintuple digits. Massive amounts of Americans are looking for a better way to control the outbreak of "LARGE GOVERNMENT DISEASE." These people want to see someone elected who believes that the small, 3 pound, 100,000,000,000 (100 billion) neuron organ that sits in the middle of our skull should be used to make good, practical decisions that will benefit the citizens of our land.

These decisions should lift our country out of debt, provide jobs for those on the dole, give us pride in our nation and prevent large swaths of the zika virus from overcoming our population.   Payton Manning understands this, he is retiring. He is taking his 18 years of experience and money and riding off into the sunset never to be seen again. He will build a large plexiglass bubble around his home so that the "Zika carrying mosquito's" can't penetrate his sphere of influence. Now that's a man who is practical.

Now here's another practical patriot,We'll try to cooperate fully with the IRS, because, as citizens, we feel a strong patriotic duty not to go to jail.

Dave Barry American columnist & humorist or as Mark Twain said "I was very particular about the kind of job I wanted. I didn't want to work. So, I went over to the Congress, that Grand Old Benevolent National Asylum for the Helpless, and I reported on the inmates there."

The problem is that last time Congress convened, this was what the whole blame opening session looked and sounded like:

The Addams Family Theme song

https://www.youtube.com/watch?v=X6QzbvH-ZNo

The country and congress needs leadership, someone who takes control, is decisive and leads us to victory.

A Soldier's Pledge with Ronald Reagan

https://www.youtube.com/watch?v=ADoq7HVmRMk

Watch out America, here comes "The Real Donald"
Carry on till tomorrow!

The Real Donald 

VOLUME 1

CHAPTER 15

The Donald Campaign Message

Trouble

03/13/2016

Yep, that's it! I finally figured out why we're having so much trouble with this election year cycle.

We've crossed the summit, we've reached the boiling point, we've eaten all of the Blue coated M & M's, we've "fiddled why Rome burned", Not familiar with this phrase? Well, here it comes….(According to a well-known expression, Rome's emperor at the time, the decadent and unpopular Nero, "fiddled while Rome burned." The expression has a double meaning: Not only did Nero play music while his people suffered, but he was an ineffectual leader in a time of crisis. Sound familiar?

Our country has been overtaken by CONTRARIANS, not aliens, CONTRARIANS! Who are they? A person who opposes or rejects popular opinion. One who goes against the current practice. According to Patricia Jones who wrote an article in the Deseret News, on March 13th, they are "popping up in national polls in today's volatile political election process." She calls these Contrarians, "C.A.V.E.s, Citizens Against Virtually Everything" and here's what's interesting. She says the research indicates, " that older men were consistently more likely to fall into the C.A.V. E. category." That puts me square in the middle of the C.A.V.E.s. Alas! another great reason to vote for me.

Here's a couple of guys from an old T.V. show in the 70's that were contrarians. Watch this:

The Odd Couple - Felix I Just Won A Car

https://www.youtube.com/watch?v=FLxS6MvHF44

I'm pretty convinced that the number of C.A.V.E.s in America is growing exponentially because they had to write "antidisestablishmentarianism", which is 28 letters long, on the blackboard of their classrooms when they were kids. After all, that is cruel and unusual punishment for some 8 year old kid, who got caught sending paper airplanes out of the second story window at school.

And, you know what's making voters more frustrated? Antidisestablishmentarianism isn't even the longest word in the English language. There is a word that is 189,819 letters long and takes a person three and a half hours to pronounce it correctly. (It's the chemical name of titin,a giant protein) according to Patricia Jones. Holy Cow! Who thought of that?

You see, we just have a bunch of grumpy people running around our streets, wondering if any of our nations issues can be fixed. They are Citizens Against Virtually Everything because they're angry from their elementary school days and worse yet, now, our politicians can't even decide whether or not to keep daylight savings time.
As I traverse this great nation, from small town to small town, I encounter people who actually know how to fix problems. After all, they can fix tractors, and rockets. They repair people and animals. They even know how to screw light bulbs into a socket, as opposed to some of our politicians, why can't we gather their ideas and solve some of our woes. Bring them back to Washington D.C. for a couple of hours, they'll solve our problems, and we can send all of the politicians home to write, I'm sorry" on the blackboard 189,819 times for misleading all of the people who voted for him/her. Thanks for fixing nothing while you were in office.

If elected, I will find the problem solvers, solve the problems one by one, and allow people to be Happy, Happy, Happy.

https://www.youtube.com/watch?v=iWp1VOFQxKg

Vote for the REAL DONALD alias C.A.V.E (man)

VOLUME 1

CHAPTER 16

The Donald Campaign Message

Clock is Ticking

03/20/2016

Fellow Citizens…

The pedal's to the metal, time's running out, the ink is drying in the well!

Yes, the numbers are dwindling by the day. At first we had a gazillion, and now, we are down to a few. Only the strong survive!

The Race is to the finish and our Rambo Chariot is showing strong. Just watch:

Ben Hur's Famous Chariot Race Scene

https://www.youtube.com/watch?v=etqvY6LmuQM

We know what the people want and they are cheering us on to victory! Listen to them:

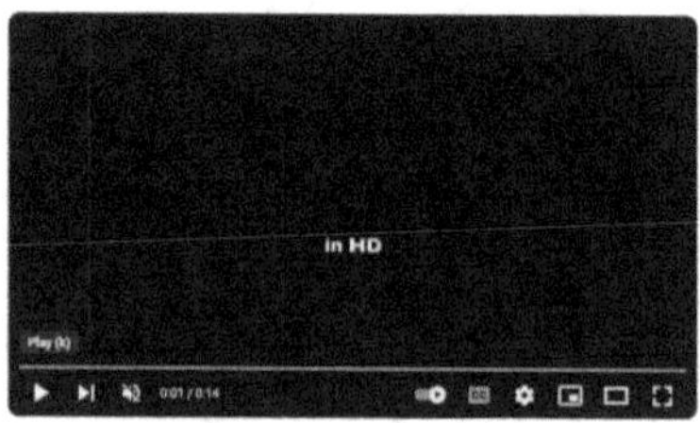

Big Crowd Cheering- sound effect

https://www.youtube.com/watch?v=Jd-22sVAryY

As the number of candidates slowly reduces, the populace coalesces around a worthy few. When asked what they are looking for in a candidate, the voters of the country, much like those surveyed in Utah, say they are looking for "a candidate who would restore America to values they believe it has lost." Deseret News, March 20,2016. They also know what they don't want, some more of the wasteful spending like what we see in China:

There's a 70-acre complex in Shanghai that's modeled after the Pentagon. But where the U.S. version is a bustling hive of national defense work, China's version is basically abandoned.

The Pentagonal Mart cost $200 million to build and was finished in 2009. Today, though, it's a rare sight to see someone cruising the aisles of canned. It's basically become the biggest vacant building in the city. People's Daily News cites the Pentagonal Mart's "location and its confusing inner structures" as the main sources of trouble. Which, yeah, I can think of places I'd rather get lost than a creepy derelict mall.

Have our taxes in the U.S. ever been spent on something like this?

Our politicians spend, talk, spend some more, talk some more and finally decide that they've spent too much. At this point, they point their fingers at the other party and say "you're to blame, for this mess we're in."

Roger Ramjet understands, here's a short conversation between him and his general:

Roger Ramjet: "General, listen. What's that?

General G.I. Brassbottom: "It's either turkeys gobbling or Congress is back in session." 93

Yes, they are in session, "Congress has approved some version of this fiscal cliff bill thing. Well, taxes are going up, and now, they're looking to make cuts just about everywhere.

In fact, oil companies today had to lay off 15 senators." Jay Leno

Did you notice that prior to the super bowl, there were weeks of coverage. Both teams, every player, their likes, dislikes. Statistics were thrown around like footballs. Every blade of grass or turf was counted and inspected by the press. We knew more about those players, how much they made,what they did and what they said about each other (which wasn't very nice, sometimes) than we know about those we elect to office. And here's the big news, WE CARE MORE ABOUT THE SUPERBOWL AND THE PLAYERS THAN WE DO ABOUT WHAT CONGRESS DOES WITH OUR MONEY AND COUNTRY.

May be something wrong here. What do our Founding Father's Think? What did the Founding Fathers want for America?
richardinman | 17 March, 2012 16:13

If more Americans pondered this simple question they would have a more clear understanding of why those brave men who came before us risked their blood, treasure and sacred honor to create the greatest nation on Earth.

The Founding Fathers were a revolutionary group, diverse in their professions and yet unified in their goal: American liberty.

They understood that the citizens should have a say in their government and that the government only derives its legitimate power from the consent of the governed.

When Thomas Jefferson penned those timeless, eloquent words of freedom in the Declaration of Independence it sent political shock waves around the world that continue to reverberate in the minds of revolutionaries everywhere.

"We hold these truths to be self-evident, that all men are created equal, that they are endowed by their Creator with certain unalienable Rights, that among these are Life, Liberty and the pursuit of Happiness. — That to secure these rights, Governments are instituted among Men, deriving their just powers from the consent of the governed, — That whenever any Form of Government becomes destructive of these ends, it is the Right of the People to alter or to abolish it, and to institute new Government, laying its foundation on such principles and organizing its powers in such form, as to them shall seem most likely to effect their Safety and Happiness."

A challenge was issued that kings did not automatically have supreme authority.

Rights come from Nature's God and it was time for men to rise up to secure these rights at any cost because it was the right thing to do. If Americans truly want the Republic that their forefathers bled for, they must educate themselves on what the Founding Fathers wanted for America and fight to restore that vision through strict adherence and respect for the Constitution.

•They must stop trading liberty for security.
•They must stop thinking the role of the government is to be involved in all aspects of their lives.
•They must take a good look at what the proper role of government is.
•They must understand that as government expands, liberty contracts.
•That government is best, which governs least.

Thomas Jefferson, a true literary warrior for American liberty, stated:

"I predict future happiness for Americans if they can prevent the government from wasting the labors of the people under the pretense of taking care of them."
Did you catch the phrase above, "IT WAS THE RIGHT THING TO DO"

There you have it. My philosophy about governing America. That phrase and the 5 bullet points above from Richard Dinman capture the essence of good leadership for our country.

In conclusion, I will share 2 prominent ideas I learned by going to church today.

1) You don't see hearses pulling U-Hauls, with worldly possessions, to heaven.

2) You can't fatten up the hog on the day of the fair.

Think about those 2 concepts and you'll outwit any of my political rivals.
Let's take the advice from above and vote for the right person, because it's the right thing to do.

Vote; The REAL DONALD 

VOLUME 1

CHAPTER 17

The Donald Campaign Message

Well Hello

03/27/2016

Throughout the country, "Inquiring Minds want to Know," What in the World is happening around here. Have you had people say, "I've never seen anything like this," This is the weirdest political year ever," "Where is this country headed?" "

Well HELLO!

Adele - Hello (Official Music Video)

https://www.youtube.com/watch?v=YQHsXMglC9A

Hang on to your hat!

Hang on to your hat. Hang on to your hope. And wind the clock, for tomorrow is another day.

THE SKY ISN'T FALLING…………IT'S JUST SUSPENDED IN OUTER DARKNESS FOR A WHILE! There is hope.

Kelby, our future "Secretary of Labor" showed us:

Age-Appropriate Chores for Children

Ages 2-3
- ☐ Put toys in toy box
- ☐ Stack books on shelf
- ☐ Place dirty clothes in laundry hamper
- ☐ Throw trash away
- ☐ Carry firewood
- ☐ Fold washcloths
- ☐ Set the table
- ☐ Fetch diapers & wipes
- ☐ Dust baseboards

Ages 4-5
- ☐ Feed pets
- ☐ Wipe up spills
- ☐ Put away toys
- ☐ Make the bed
- ☐ Straighten bedroom
- ☐ Water houseplants
- ☐ Sort clean silverware
- ☐ Prepare simple snacks
- ☐ Use hand-held vacuum
- ☐ Clear kitchen table
- ☐ Dry and put away dishes
- ☐ Disinfect doorknobs

Ages 6-7
- ☐ Gather trash
- ☐ Fold towels
- ☐ Dust mop floors
- ☐ Empty dishwasher
- ☐ Match clean socks
- ☐ Weed garden
- ☐ Rake leaves
- ☐ Peel potatoes or carrots
- ☐ Make salad
- ☐ Replace toilet paper roll

Ages 8-9
- ☐ Load dishwasher
- ☐ Change light bulbs
- ☐ Wash laundry
- ☐ Hang/fold clean clothes
- ☐ Dust furniture
- ☐ Spray off patio
- ☐ Put groceries away
- ☐ Scramble eggs
- ☐ Bake cookies
- ☐ Walk dogs
- ☐ Sweep porches
- ☐ Wipe off tables

Ages 10-11
- ☐ Clean bathrooms
- ☐ Vacuum rugs
- ☐ Clean countertops
- ☐ Deep clean kitchen
- ☐ Prepare simple meal
- ☐ Mow lawn
- ☐ Bring in mail
- ☐ Do simple mending (hems, buttons, etc.)
- ☐ Sweep out garage

Ages 12 and up
- ☐ Mop floors
- ☐ Change overhead lights
- ☐ Wash/vacuum car
- ☐ Trim hedges
- ☐ Paint walls
- ☐ Shop for groceries w/list
- ☐ Cook complete dinner
- ☐ Bake bread or cake
- ☐ Do simple home repairs
- ☐ Wash windows
- ☐ Iron clothes
- ☐ Watch younger siblings

So, those on the dole, really can work.   See age appropriate chores for all age groups.
Here's a couple of ideas:

We need people to feed the pets…This dog loves peanut butter!

Dog Eating Peanut Butter – YouTube

Dog Eating Peanut Butter

https://www.youtube.com/watch?v=qh4DATEKFLc

and here's a man who has made the most from his talents: Homeless Man Plays Piano Beautifully (Sarasota, FL …)

https://www.youtube.com/watch?v=JCguq3hTC2M
NOTE at the time of publishing this video was no longer available.

So, what's the message for this week? If a person has a need, let's address it, let them work, in some way to pay for it, and then let them have the respect to get back to a fulfilling way of life.
Any time the country tries to do everything for everybody, the country ends up doing nothing for nobody.   We all loose!
Let's fix this mess shall we?

Vote for the REAL DONALD 

VOLUME 1

CHAPTER 18

The Donald Campaign Message

Madness of March

04/03/2016

As March Madness concludes, the hopes, aspirations and plain old "good luck" (think Syracuse) of all the teams comes to an end. There are only two teams left to enter the final match. Which one will come out victorious?

At the beginning of this campaign, there were 17 candidates who wanted to be the next President of the United Sates of America. Now, we have the "Surreal Six." Surreal, you say? Yes, having the qualities of surrealism; bizarre.

"a surreal mix of fact and fantasy"

Synonyms: unreal, bizarre, unusual, weird, strange, freakish, unearthly, uncanny, dreamlike, phantasmagorical

PHANTASMAGORICAL? That's the perfect word for this election year!

Here's a basic look at the six remaining candidates: (Click on the pictures below and then go to the link below the picture)

The Addams Family TV Show Opening 1964 – YouTube

Herman Munster tries out for the Dodgers – YouTube

Still, the other 5 candidates fail to consider the burning questions that are at the top of all our citizens minds. For example; " A spinning top always stops. Why does the Earth keep spinning?" Our citizens are concerned. What if the Earth quits spinning. Can the next president handle this issue?

It's essential that a potential President can address these issues to alleviate any fear that may prevent the public from doing their daily chores like chopping pickles for canning. Without pickles, all major hamburger joints shut down and everyone starves to death because no one knows how to cook a homemade meal anymore.

Here are some of the other major concerns on the minds of Americans:

Near 20-Year High: Bee-pocalypse Postponed Again, Until 2017
California Drought Patterns Becoming More Common
What does a physicist do in his/her spare time?
Ancient DNA Shows European Wipe-out Of Early Americans

The Top Quark Mass In 2016

Only the "Real Donald" is aware of these concerns and has a platform to address and solve these issues. Next week we will address these issues.

Now a member of my campaign staff will give the Pledge of Allegiance to show how we will start every meeting in the White House and Congress if I am elected. (Make sure you watch it until the end, it's only 4:20 minutes.

Red Skelton's Pledge of Allegiance – YouTube

That's it folks, have a happy and prosperous week!

Vote for the REAL DONALD 

VOLUME 1

CHAPTER 19

The Donald Campaign Message

What They Said….What They Meant

04/10/2016

I saw the other day that the Feds (The Federal Reserve Board) which is made up of our brightest economists (3) and lawyers (2) and vacancies (2) have decided not to raise the federal interest rate. Now, I was quite surprised in December, after not raising the rate during the financial crisis, they decided to raise the rate by a quarter of a percent.

Now, they say nope, we were wrong, the Ouija Board,Tea leaves and Crystal Ball we were using developed a bad case of the Zika Virus. We have now returned to throwing darts at the dart board, in hopes that we can get this thing right at least 50% of the time instead of missing the target entirely.

What the Fed said:
In determining the timing and size of future adjustments to the target range for the federal funds rate, the Committee will assess realized and expected economic conditions relative to its objectives of maximum employment and 2 percent inflation. This assessment will take into account a wide range of information, including measures of labor market conditions, indicators of inflation pressures and inflation expectations, and readings on financial and international developments. In light of the current shortfall of inflation from 2 percent, the Committee will carefully monitor actual and expected progress toward its inflation goal.

What the Fed meant:
We're not just making this up as we go along. There are numbers — so many numbers — and we're watching them all to decide when to raise rates. Want labor numbers? We got 'em. Inflation expectations data? We've got you covered.

Alan Graf/Cultura/Getty Images

These are the files they use as a backdrop for their dartboard.

I am pretty sure that Meterologists would score higher on Advanced Placement tests than Federal Reserve Board members. When is the last time you listened to your weather person with any degree of reliance? So, Economist's and Government officials, with whopping degrees are no smarter than the average American citizen. Only thieves have a better success rate because they have found a way to bilk the system and make money by taking from others.

What does this have to do with a political campaign? Well, the President appoints the Chairman and the Vice Chairman of the Federal Reserve board. My appointees for both positions would be ONE Fortune Teller and ONE Las Vegas Roulette Dealer. Watch this economy soar! The banter between candidates keeps rising. It's reaching a boiling point.

https://www.youtube.com/watch?v=uRDNLTMaZqo
NOTE: At the time of publishing the video was no longer available.

All of the remaining candidates sound a bit like this to those who now have to choose a candidate for America.

<u>Hilarious dog talking at the start of dog sled race –</u>
<u>YouTube</u>

Just remember, "You can't fatten up the hog on the day of the fair!

Vote The "REAL Donald" 

VOLUME 1

CHAPTER 20

The Donald Campaign Message

The Course is Set

04/17/2016

The course has been set. The ship has left the dock and the sailors are singing the words above as they set sail for the new land. It seems like uncharted territory but, in reality, there is a compass, there are stars and there are plenty of signs to tell us which way to go. We just need to listen to the words of nature, aka the "still small voice."

In the 2016 presidential campaign there is a similar ring coming from the bell tower. The people of the country are sending a message but, no one listens to the faint tones whispering across our land.

We are seeing a polarization of the citizens. Some are saying, "I'm fed up with the bickering, the indecisiveness, the inability to accomplish even a menial task within the Congress or the Executive Branch.

Most Important Problem Facing the U.S. in 2015

Issues averaging 2% or higher

	Yearly average^	Highest monthly result	Lowest monthly result
	%	%	%
Government/Congress/Politicians	16	19	13
Economy in general	13	17	9
Unemployment/Jobs	8	11	6
Immigration	8	12	5
Healthcare	6	10	3
Ethics/Moral decline	5	7	3
Race relations/Racism	5	9	3
Terrorism	5	16	2
Federal budget deficit/Federal debt	5	7	2
Education	5	7	3
Poverty/Hunger/Homelessness	3	5	2
National security	3	5	2
Gap between rich and poor	3	4	2
Crime/Violence	3	6	1
Foreign aid/Focus overseas	3	4	2
Situation in Iraq/ISIS	3	6	1
Judicial system/Courts/Laws	2	4	1
Environment/Pollution	2	3	1
Guns/Gun control	2	7	0
Lack of respect for each other	2	3	1
Lack of money	2	3	1
International issues or problems	2	3	1
Wars/War (non-specific)/Fear of War	2	2	1

^Based on average of 12 monthly surveys

Holy Cow! You mean to tell me that "THE GOVERNMENT" is the biggest problem in America? Why yes, according to this Gallup Poll. And a U.S. News and World Report dated Jan. 3, 2016 had "THE GOVERNMENT" listed as the #2 problem, just one percentage point behind Unemployment. The U.S. News article had it listed as "Dissatisfaction with government/Congress/politicians;

poor leadership/corruption/abuse of power.

Well now folks, how do we fix this problem? Let's see, here are some examples from our previous presidents. President George Washington refused to accept his presidential salary, which was $25,00 a year. That sent a nice message to the citizens. His inauguration speech was the shortest on record —133 words and less than two minutes long. Doesn't sound like the verbose candidates running for office today. Now contrast that 133 words with William Henry Harrison who holds the record for the longest inauguration speech in history at 8,578 words long and one hour and 40 minutes. Unfortunately, he gave the speech during bad weather and a month later, he was dead from pneumonia, making his the shortest presidency on record. Whoa! I think there is foreboding message there?

On his epitaph, which he composed, Jefferson mentions that he was the author of the Declaration of Independence and the statuette of Virginia for Religious Freedom. He did not mention that he had been the President of the United States. Probably, a sign of humility, rare among modern day presidents and candidates.

Barack Obama collects Spiderman and Conan the Barbarian comic books. (not sure what this tells us but you can read into it (pun intended) as you like!
So, where is all of this leading my campaign this week. When you get a few minutes, take a look at this graduation speech given by David McCullough (son of the renown author David McCullough Sr. who wrote 1776). This talk is meant for any and all politicians today. My message to them from the campaign trail is; "Your are not Special."

You Are Not Special Commencement Speech from ...

▶ 12:46

*https://www.**you**tube.com/watch?v=_IfxYhtf8o4*

Vote the Real Donald 

VOLUME 1

Appendix

I would like to submit my application for the position of Secretary of Defense Against Booers. As Secretary of Defense Against Booers I will ensure that swift and consistent justice is applied to all people who boo at inappropriate times. All those booing at inappropriate times shall face the consequences of a partial justice system, which in layman's terms means a nice kick to the pants. In order to carry out these measures we will have Professional Pantskickers who are six sigma, alpha beta epsilon, omega 3, blackbelt, and Kung Fu Panda qualified to fulfill these important positions. We will begin poring through applications immediately upon designation and expect to have all positions filled by the time we leave office in 4 to 8 years, GST (Government Standard Time).

The Real Donald doesn't build walls, he tears them down

-To a More Perfect Union

We are all well aware that Donald Trump and Hillary Clinton are the leading candidates for President of the United States, but please take a step back and consider another candidate, one who is better qualified to serve as our Commander-in-Chief. His name is the Real Donald, and as the first and only person to unify the Continental Divide, quantify the English language, and extract aloe vera form a maple tree, he is at least worth your consideration. Thank you.

Vote the Real Donald!!

-Brandon Perry

The Donald will ride again...